She Hears The Wind

CHERYL KNOLL

Printed in the United States of America

ISBN 979-8-89114-052-3 (sc)
ISBN 979-8-89114-053-0 (hc)
ISBN 979-8-89114-054-7 (e)

Library of Congress Control Number: 2024901367

2024.01.22

MainSpring Books
5901 W. Century Blvd
Suite 750
Los Angeles, CA, US, 90045

www.mainspringbooks.com

Contents

She Hears The Wind 1

The Source 2

Love in The Woods 3

Stay The Course 4

Nice Advice 5

Drifting Snow 6

Earth's Crowning Jewel 7

While The Neighbors Sleep 8

Grounded 9

God Sees 10

Autumn's Army 11

God's Hedge 12

Throw Away Throne 13

Smelting Pot 14

Wind's Song 15

Without God 16

Crazy Love 17

A World with No More Politics 18

Moving Forward 19

Real Value 20

God's Caretakers 21

Blow in The Red Pills 22

They Marched 23

Tightrope in The Fog 25

Thread to Rope..26

Let Go..27

Background Music..28

The Fake President...29

Internal Voice Choice...30

Learn God's Way 31

Fix Your Heart 32

Her Savoir-faire Slipped 33

Falling, Drifting..34

In Favor of Density..35

I Will Pass...36

The Losing Lesson 37

Breaking Trees Break Hearts 38

A Weak Stink..39

God's Trees 40

Don't Take a Hit..41

Flat Earth 42

Worthy Man..43

Last Warning 44

The Moon Mirror 45

Love is Stronger..46

Desire 47

Your Bodyguard 48

God's Inheritance..49

Host with The Most...50

Wind of Change..51

Silver Stream...53

Walk Through 54

Take A Step Back.. 55

Welcoming Committee.. 56

Treat Yourself.. 57

Such as These.. 58

Old Man Winter 59

When a Strong Man Cries 60

Frank and Ludmilla 62

Silent Winter Night... 64

Keep Hold of My Hand 65

The Rock Tumbler 66

Life Happens... 67

Remember Your Baby?....................................... 68

The Lord is My Holiday 70

Do not Give Your Power Away 71

Justice.. 73

God's Fire 75

Snow Love... 76

Summer Evening 77

Wisdom Calls.. 78

God's Lonely Heart Club................................... 79

True Friend 80

Shut The Door 81

His Son 82

Too Many Voices 83

Shade is A Shadow 84

Who's Watching Who?.. 85

Tarnish Remover..86

Checking Out Trees...87

Soldier for The Lord..89

Halo of Feathers...90

God's Cheerleaders 91

Chocolate Secret..92

Windy Visit...93

Happy in The Now Space 94

I Know This Tree...95

Get The Rake...96

Larry and Rose 97

Counting Fake Feathers 98

Stay Busy Not Lazy 99

Accept The Invitation 100

Look Beyond Seeing.......................................101

Clarence...102

Full Moon 103

Going Downhill... 104

Two is Company 106

Horse Smiles..107

Changing Instruments 108

Pebbles to Mountains 109

Feeding The Soul... 110

Water Trees 111

Clouds of Birds.. 112

Be Yourself 113

The Slow Down Gift.......................................114

Gentle Love...116

Stir The Flame...117

Oh-No...118

Grab The Tailwind...119

It is Good to Be Home 120

Celebrate Honesty..121

Really Real 122

The Greatest Shelter 123

Mourning Coffee..124

The Cardinal's Song..125

End The Movie 126

Respect for The Elderly 127

No Rain 128

Praying Late..129

Be Well Rooted 130

The Wings I Loved 131

Beautiful Wine...132

Gust 133

Walk Slow 134

No Thank You...135

Slippery Slope..136

Snow Geese...137

The Gift of Love...138

Ascending 139

Oldie but Goodie 140

Compassionate Wind..141

Blackbird Leaves 142

The Show 143

Truth Seeker 144

Invisible Wind...145

Hold Your Vision..146

Killing Flowers 147

Be Strong 148

She Hears The Wind

She hears the wind, inside she sighs

For now, her flower world dies

It was disappointing, the loss

Her heart has changed, no flowers

Now moss

Her love of flowers comes to an end

Gone in the winds, no more to tend

She hears the wind and its powerful cry

No more would flowers live under her sky

There was a shift, it changed her plan

She hears the wind berating man

She tells the wind she understands

He must do this, it is out of her hands

Blow wind blow, blow up, blow down

Blow to the cities, the country, the town

Shake up man and make him think

While you are at it, blow out the stink

Her flowers now, a memory

The wind is blowing

She can see

The Source

Who can understand the wind's ways?

From where it comes and where it goes

Where it begins, where it ends

God is the only one who knows

Though while it is traveling unseen

It searches for those whose ears are keen

Alas, the ears that hear are rare

When found, being grateful, it will share

You will learn things you did not know

The wind can be your friend or foe

Deep things, knowing ears will hear

Special words to keep, they will stay near

The one with the power to control that force

The beautiful words, come from that source

Love in The Woods

In the woods, him, and her

Under towering trees, they felt a stir

Birds sat quiet, the breeze was low

Deer looked on, they walked by slow

He loved her and she loved him

In the evening when the sun was dim

He reached out, she took his hand

They stood and kissed in the wooded land

He was strong like the trees

She was soft, like the breeze

Deep in the woods

They stood like trees

Loves roots were strong

They prayed Lord please

Keep our love pure and deep

Now the trees have a secret to keep

Stay The Course

The tide had turned

My ship had tipped

I stayed the course

Though my feet slipped

Though my feet slipped

I did not fall

The waves were stilled

With God's own call

Ships do not always have smooth sailing

When winds of change become prevailing

Sea legs learn the waters ways

The soul's compass, leads us to God's days

Nice Advice

At times, the wind was fairly nice
Offering up some good advice
To make me whole, to make me good
To live the way, I knew I should
It spoke
"Never share your personal life
Things others do not need to know
Happily, mind your own business
Then your peace will always show
Let no emotions overpower you
Be still and quiet and count to four
If you still cannot keep control
Go ahead and count some more
Silence prevents many ills
Keeping secrets brings great thrills
Stop thinking everyone is your friend
Questionable friendships need to end
Listen more, let your words be few
You will find these make a better you
No more judging, look for good
No criticizing, unless you should"
I spoke in return
"Sometimes wind, you blow my mind
When it comes to friends
You are one of a kind"

Drifting Snow

Staring at the drifting snow
It wants to fall, though the wind makes it blow
Snow has a destiny, a chosen path
Wind can be a breeze or a fury with wrath

Hence, two forces with agendas of their own
The will of the weaker can be overthrown
There will still be beautiful sights to see
Drifts of snow, forms the wind set free

The wind will subside and let falling snow fall
When the snow has its way, it will cover all
Just as the ways of nature are keen
There are God's ways, some yet to be seen

Sometimes I am falling snow
Sometimes I drift where God's Spirit makes me go
At times I have melted, at times I have been frozen
I do what God asks of me; it is His ways I have chosen

For as much as I love to watch snow fall
Even more than that, I listen for God's call

Earth's Crowning Jewel

Trees were dancing, horses prancing

Birds flying upside down

Flowers exploded in full bloom

With a glimpse of Christ's white gown

Crops in the fields burst with grain

Fish and water mammals leapt

Wild animals stood on two legs

Nothing on earth slept

The air was now charged with God's power

Jesus Christ returned to rule

All creation gave God glory

Our Lord is here, earth's crowning jewel

All creation gave God praise

Church bells rang for many days

The clouds all fled, it was a sight

To see the shining of God's light

Every knee bowed down to earth

Every person felt their worth

The Lord is here, the Lord is near

His spoken words, we will hold dear

His ears will hear us all confess

Jesus Christ is Lord to the glory of God

Jesus Christ is Lord

While The Neighbors Sleep

While the neighbors are sleeping

It is late, and I am awake

Reflecting upon my day with the Lord

What did I give, what did I take?

I think on what I have done

I hope I was not slack

I am remembering everything God gave me today

Wondering what I can give back

Today was one of those days for me

I felt God's hand, and I could see

Something I prayed for coming to fruition

It was all God, not my intuition

His Holy Spirit fills my soul

Some trying days had taken their toll

Lord, I wish others could feel and see

How you bless those who live for thee

Lord, I offer my love to you

Prayers, blessings, and praises too

Lord if there is anything I can do

While the neighbors are sleeping

I am here with you

Grounded

Taking in earth's energy
Bare feet standing on the ground
The earth is God's, with healing powers
In bare feet I have found

When grounded feet wear shoes
They beg to shed to bare
To stand in grass or in the dirt
On God's earth, anywhere

There is a power that you cannot see
God's earth is full of energy
Like medicine, that you can feel
In bare feet, you will find it is real

The earth is calling out to you
Take your shoes off now my friend
Get yourself grounded with bare feet
Too tired to stand, sit on your rear-end

God Sees

Where the wild roses grow
And where the trees give way to skies
Dark skies wear a billion stars
Landscape twinkles with fireflies

Birds are nestled in the trees
Nocturnal creatures roam about
The only sound, the hoot of an owl
Happy for night, no doubt

Where the wild roses grow
God's eyes see the roses show
He is omnipresent, he sees it all
He sees the petals when they fall

The stars are numbered, he knows them all
He sees the fireflies and hears the owl call
God has his eyes also on you
He knows everything you do

Do things to help; let goodness show
He sees you everywhere you go
Like stars or fireflies, shine your light
Bloom like roses in his sight

Bloom when no one else can see
He will let you see eternity

Autumn's Army

A battalion of leaves

Charging across the street

Like little soldiers

They received their marching orders

From the wind

Reinforcements follow

Troops from the right flank

A platoon from the left

Recruits follow

To set up base camp

In the neighbor's yard

Finders' keepers

God's Hedge

Protect me Lord, in precarious times

All around, humankind is falling
All around, humankind is straying
Their ears are not open, to hear you calling
Their lips on their faces do not do any praying

Your hedge of protection surrounding me
Comforting Lord, for I live for thee
The straying and falling who come my way
Your protecting hedge keeps me safe as I pray

Though any straying and falling I see
I will pray for them Lord, and how can it be
Their ears cannot hear your beautiful culling
My prayer can help prevent them from falling

Throw Away Throne

She sat a queen, enthroned in her stuff

Boxes, bags, and clothes piled high

Papers, bottles, trash, and food

Piles of rodent feces nearby

She had stained bedding

Stained clothes, old shoes

Newspapers with twenty-year-old news

Dishes with roaches and rotting food

She slept like a dog, her bed was crude

She could not part with rotting trash

She piled it high, it was her stash

Then, she was outed, and someone knew

Now wondering how these piles grew

Some people thought she was crazy

Others thought that she was lazy

Her mind had clicked off long ago

That helped to make the piles grow

Inside she had a troubled heart

Now things she touched, no more to part

Her mind and heart now felt protected

Hiding in filth, others rejected

Mental illness, no one sees

She lives in trash above her knees

It is a strange and sad disorder

This poor woman, was a hoarder

Smelting Pot

Some tried to rule with an invisible iron hand
They met their match with the smelting pot
Their plans to rule could not come to fruition
For God's peoples pot was hot

Godless people who served Satan's throne
Exposed with their plans, they were thrown in the fire
Their crimes against humanity caused the pot to burst
Evil exploded and the flames went higher

Crimes so evil, seared the good people's minds
The evil that was caused could not be forgotten
The evil ones executed, caused people to rejoice
Never to live again, so evil and rotten

They thought they had power, they wanted to rule
Government, businesses, and every school
They wanted all people under their control
But the righteous had shovels and dug a big hole

In the hole, the smelting pot simmers on low
To remind the people which way they should go
Should they turn back to evil and let us hope not
The fire still burns, and we will keep the pot hot

Wind's Song

Their ears were open to wind's song
Singing of where man went wrong
There is a fixing in the air
There is a fixing, wind will swear
Wind uses trees to hit notes higher
This time it will not invite the fire
Though maybe it will change its mind
If there are no hearing ears to find

Without God

See Satan, luring the weak
Without God, they are all fair game
Truth has no place in their lives
Satan knows them all by name
Oh dear, just mention God, they cringe
They scream and their saliva flows
They cling to and push sexuality
Preferring lies, while mayhem grows
Abortion gives them evil pleasure
Abusing children without measure
They have turned themselves into a show
Now, evident where they will go
So sad to see IQ's so low
Hearts so cold and brains so slow
These are those who Satan rules
He trains them young in public schools
A wicked and perverse generation
God warned us of them in His word
They will fall along with Satan
For rejecting God, His words not heard
Still God calls and some will turn
Those who hate God, they will burn
Stay away from those falling away
All you can do now, is pray

Crazy Love

When your higher self and your lower self are at war
You may feel as though your insides tore
Your mind takes on a life of its own
The only thing you can be is alone
You pray to God for a word or a sign
Though nothing comes from Him, our divine
And still the feelings are ripping apart
What is left
When you cannot control your heart
Like the wind that ravages the land
And leaves a breeze and you still stand
Confused
Falling in love, Lord
Can feel like being abused

"Be still and know I am" God spoke
Love never is or was a joke
Divine timing works its own way
You can feel crazy, or you can pray
Make no mistake
You are coming to the day
True love will show and
It is coming to stay

A World with No More Politics

I dream of a world with no more politics

Where our leaders are appointed by God

With no more lies told by politicians

Where we have executed the evil sod

No more to be blinded by delusion

No more to live in a state of confusion

Where we are not being robbed of every right

Where we live in goodness in God's sight

With no suppression we are free

Living the life God meant to be

I dream of a world where Christ is our King

We love him so much, all people will sing

Then words from politicians, no more to be spoken

No more promises designed to be broken

Where we live by God's laws everyday

The people would not have it any other way

Where God's rewards for us are great

Where evil is the only thing, we will hate

Dear God, I know my prayers are heard

I love you and I love your word

I dream of the world that you will fix

When we are ruled by you with no politics

Moving Forward

Put your best foot forward
Then bring your other foot from behind
Then your other foot becomes your best foot
With two moving feet you will find
Your feet will walk a path forward
Moving forward is better than staying
The only time you should stop on your path
Is when you are on your knees praying

Real Value

She did not need a ring or jewels

She did not need expensive schools

She did not care for a social life

She shook her head at worldly strife

She spent her time on things of God

She highly revered his guiding rod

Nothing in this world could take His place

It was to His ways, she kept her face

She would sit in the dark of night

She prayed that she was living right

She prayed if there was something to do

To give it to her, she would see it through

Her love for God to her was great

She prayed to God, and she would wait

For God to give her or show her things

She valued that more than jewelry or rings

God's Caretakers

God loves his caretakers
Providing animals with care
Nourishment and medical care
With a friendly hand that is fair
Keepers of animals in pastures
Caretakers for those in pens
Those who watch and protect from predators
God sees you in his lens

God has others in his lens
They will be accountable on judgement day
Cruelly caring for or barely feeding
With no comforting place to lay
The man who has stockpiles of feed
His cattle are in winter pastures, thin
A lazy man clinging to a dollar bill
Starving animals, to God that is sin

Starved dogs wearing heavy chains
Horses starving with no feed
Cattle bawling, thin with hunger
You do not care for your animals in need
Try explaining your actions to God
It is not going to go your way
God hates to see suffering animals
Every dog will have its day

Blow in The Red Pills

People were looking for relief

Unfortunately, the wind was chief

Blowing words at incredible speeds

Those with ears could hear its needs

When God said there would be few chosen

He was right, the masses are frozen

Locked in ice blocks made of lies

Their hearts will not thaw, they have blind eyes

Devolution will be their demise

Their goblets are full, they are drunk on lies

Just when you think they must be full

They cannot stop drinking in all the bull

Enough is enough is enough is enough

Now someone is serving up bullshit fluff

When? Oh, when will they wake? You ask

It is past time to see what is under the mask

With hearing ears, we shake our heads

Take the red pills now, sleepers

Take the truth meds

They Marched

The righteous people linked their arms
They formed a chain to make a stand
Strong they stood, and strong they marched
To reclaim and clean their land
They fought and cleaned the election system
Exposing fraud and arresting traitors
They fought and cleaned the colleges
Ousting Marxists, the freedom haters

They fought and cleaned their children's schools
Removing Teachers Union orders
No more dividing skin colors by race
No teaching sex or gender disorders
They marched and fought the media
Starting networks that reported truth
The network hosts reported honestly
The fastest growing segment watching, was our youth

The people marched and cleaned up morals
They put sex back where it belonged
The media changed what it projected
It righted what was wronged
You see, people had become nauseated
With endless sex shoved in their face
It was part of Satan's plan
To take God's natural plan out of place

They marched and fought pedophilia
No more children would be raped
They fought and executed pedophiles
Damnation to any who had escaped
They marched and fought the abortion industry
Never again would the unborn be killed
Women would carry their babies full term
They will give birth and feel fulfilled

They fought and cleaned the political system
No more would politicians' rule and reign
Once more the politicians worked for the people
With a modest salary and no exorbitant gain
The political system was refined
The government, the people greatly downsized
States had their own responsibilities
Government was tolerable again, all surmised

When the righteous link their arms with God's
It is a power that cannot be broken
With their marching legs and cleaning arms
With their mouths, God's words were spoken

Tightrope in The Fog

When you walk a tightrope in the fog
And your balancing pole is as limp as string
And the wind is blowing like a storm
And you cannot see or feel anything

Why the hell are you walking on that rope?
When you could be walking solid ground
Take one step at a time in the fog
Pray away the troubles you found
You can pray and leave them in the fog
For someone else find
Your balancing pole will get stronger with prayer
Good-bye storm
Hello peace of mind

Thread to Rope

Stuck in time, its passing stalls
You cannot get beyond the walls
A painful struggle to get ahead
Time stands still, it is all but dead

Reach your hands out to the future
Find something new and take a detour
Have a vision to see something new
A thread of vision for the future you

The future's thread when held with hope
Will turn the thread into a rope
Being stuck in time that stalls
Will help you put doors in the walls

Learning can be a looking glass
Work to the future, time will pass
New doors will open, you will see
With God, time is eternity

You held the rope God pulled you through
The hard work, it all came from you

Let Go

So sad, now it was broken
It was a cherished dish
Hope could not put it together
Neither could a wish

A mother's memories
Were ingrained in that bowl
Now it laid in many pieces
It could not be made whole

That is how things in life can be
Now it is the past, no more to see
Some things we just need to throw
When things are broken, they need to go

There may be sadness for the loss
When things in life we need to toss
When something is gone, it leaves a space
God sees the void and fills that place

Out with the old, wait for the new
God will bring something better for you

Background Music

Thank you, Lord, for ears that hear
Discerning wind can bring a fear
Though I do not fear, I am by your side
At times you reach out and confide
Yesterday, I heard wind's words
It blended with the chirping birds
What a beautiful mix of sound,
Wind, with bird songs, as background
Deciphering messages, I would find
Melodious words came to my mind
There is a gift for those who hear
My sky grew cloudy, now it is clear
Troubles just kept coming my way
Your special wind blew them away
Lord, your wind shows me my way
The path your words blow, I will stay
From your path, I will not stray
What will your wind tell me today?

The Fake President

We were overwhelmed with trouble this year

Anger brewing, we could hear

A masked man in the leader's role

Working for demise, his goal

He was under special control

He babbled words, he was not whole

The wind screamed "Fools, he is not real"

A fake election he did steal

What is in the foolish minds?

The same stuff pushed out from behinds

How can you flat out not see?

You are living in fake reality

The wind was pounding

Wind speeds abounding

What the hell will it take?

For you to see this man is fake

Eighty-one million votes, hell no

Corruption and lies

The wind will blow

Internal Voice Choice

Silently walking away inside

To something secretly calling

Some jobs are not forever jobs

When you feel your soul is stalling

The job you once loved is breaking its bond

You feel an unsettling grief

It is ok to search for a change

You can follow that inner belief

Stumbling blocks can become steppingstones

When you listen to that internal voice

You can stay and pray, or leave and believe

God will help guide you with your choice

Learn God's Way

They go to church, looking to be fed
With hungry souls, they sit on pews
Their souls long for the word of God
Though they suffer the preacher's views

Remember Jesus said feed my lambs
Remember, he said, feed my sheep
So many preachers are not feeding God's flock
They just put them to sleep

The pews are left warm, while the people leave cold
People were looking for God's word to be told
God said learn by chapters, verse by verse
Though preachers tell stories and look in your purse

The lambs are growing stunted, they are not being fed
The sheep leave church hungry; they are not being lead
Judgement will come to those who do not rightly teach
If you do not know God's word, you should not preach

Fix Your Heart

A heart holding a wall of hate
A heavy wall with too much weight
It is a heavy burden to bear
The hate and hurt you carry there

You have a tight grip on that grudge
Just let it go, our Lord will judge
Stop carrying others trash
Stop hurting your heart, hate spreads like rash

Forgiveness removes that wall of hate
Turn that wall into a gate
Open your gate and let the grudge go
Only you will have to know

You can forgive then try to forget
A new sun will rise, a better sun will set
You can do it all without anyone knowing
Love yourself now, the hate and grudges need throwing

Her Savoir-faire Slipped

She was smelling the fragrance in the breeze
Walking near a row of lilac trees
She was mourning the loss of her savoir- faire
Like the fragrance, she always had a flair

She had a natural ability
To always say and do what is right
Though now her savoir- faire had slipped
She lost her gift last night

Last night she let her morals slip
Too much wine caused too much lip
Stumbling a bit from side to side
Her savoir-faire took a downhill slide

She walked the lilacs to clear her head
She regretted last night's words she said
She took some time while in the trees
She prayed and said, "God forgive me please"

The Lord forgives and he forgets
Do not torture yourself with past regrets
She inhaled all the fragrance the lilacs could give
Today is another day and she will live

Falling, Drifting

Autumn's glory and a cloudy sky

I see the zinnias have grown so high

Beckoning trees on autumn days

I feel them calling

I hear them calling

Walk through the trees

When leaves are falling

Walk on slightly breezy days

Leaves are drifting

Drifting down

Leaves are falling, they are drifting

Down to the ground

In wonderment

I walk the trees

When leaves drift down

When there is a breeze

In Favor of Density

There was a case
In the court of common sense
The pulling force of gravity
Versus density, hence

Density accused gravity
Of being a lie and a farce
Density's claim, things heavier than air would fall
There should be no more words to parse

Gravity made a false claim
That there was a magnet
In the core of the earth
The truth of the matter, is heavy things fall
The verdict should be gravity has no worth

The judge weighed the matter
He said density was proved right
Things heavier than air would fall
The judge ruled if gravity
Could produce evidence of the magnet
His verdict, he would recall

I Will Pass

Lord, I will pass on having friends
If that is okay with you
If you do not mind, I do not want more
The ones I had I threw
You are the only friend I want
You are the only one I need
You are the only one I trust
The rest I had to weed
Acquaintances, I find are kinder
Nicer than phony friends
Friendship goes both ways, they say
Though most become dead ends

She was eating macaroni
Thinking her friends were all so phony
They were like vegetables, bitter not sweet
Not like the Lord, who fed her good meat
It was time to clean her plate
Spoiled offerings from false friends were weight
Her table now, set for the Lord
Her faithful friend, her great reward

The Losing Lesson

I told the wind

"There are so many things in this life I had to lose"

The wind said

"What is more important?

Your life or things you choose?

I will blast a fine rose as well as the trees

I am not discerning

When I encounter these

I ravage your roses as well as their thorns

I will dry up your flowers

And endure your scorns

A force has no pity for loss that it brings

That is how people learn

To survive bad things"

The wind can destroy everything

And all that you own

But you can live to stand your ground

Even if you stand alone

Breaking Trees Break Hearts

She hears the wind, and she says Lord please

I do not like the wind breaking my trees

It is sad to see trees, break, and fall

They stood so beautiful and tall

It reminds me of people who also fell

Even some strong ones did not stand well

Even the brave souls die in wars

They go down like trees when the battle roars

Trees and people, break, and fall

It breaks my heart and after all

Now there is a big mess to clean

Lord, I wish the wind would stop being mean

A Weak Stink

The wind announced its words to speak

I am sick of mortal man so weak

The strong man stands to take my blows

The weak man cries and sputters woes

I hear you wind, your blows are not kind

Weak men make me lose my mind

Their strength, a waste of what God made

The world's winds make them seek the shade

What a farce, a hoax, a joke

With sissy pants, they claim they are woke

Good Lord, dear God, where are the strong men

Wake up the woke, if not now, then when?

To join the men who have always been

Though they are few, just one in ten

Even less, amen? Amen

God's Trees

Like giant redwoods, God's people stood tall

They would not let God's America fall

They gathered the brambles choking all

They dismantled the power of the cabal

They threw the brambles in the fire

To burn to ashes as the flames went higher

No more brambles left to choke

They burned

They burned

They turned to smoke

Now, we all must clear the air

We can live free, not in despair

Our God, He is the mightiest tree

We stand like redwoods, Lord, with thee

Don't Take a Hit

Don't you love it when the shit hits the fan
You are not the one on the wrong side
You see people getting away with so much
At times, wrongdoing they cannot hide

Wrongdoers can only get away with so much
They reap what they sow, and the shit hits the fan
A good splattering for others to see
If the shit does not stop them, you can

Flat Earth

The world had spun out of control
The spin revealed the earth was flat
It did not rotate, flat earth sat still
It was the galaxy that spun as flat earth sat

Someone played an evil trick
Deceiving all, the world was round
To what extent could man be fooled
Ah yes, lies did abound

Flat earth sits still, rimmed with ice shields
It sits and waits for God's return
God looks down from heaven and speaks
That is my flat earth, it does not turn

Worthy Man

Where is a worthy man?

To lead a nation under God

To govern this nation's citizens

To care for those abroad

Where is a worthy man?

A man whose lips do not beguile

His words are truth

With an honest smile

He acknowledges God

When he speaks to the masses

He does not divide people

Into races and classes

When he looks at a man and sees a man

When something is wrong, he does everything he can

A man who openly and secretly prays

He asks God to lead and guide his ways

Where is this man, whose values have worth?

Dear Lord

Is there a man like this left on the earth?

Last Warning

The wind was blowing
The speed was set
It screamed "Do I have your attention yet?"
How much do I have to blow?
Until you know, until you know
I have destruction in my power
I am giving you another hour
To catch the truth my wind will spread
Open your eyes you walking dead
Earthly things that hold your minds
Bodily decorations of all kinds
Your ears are closed when truth is spoken
Your bond with God is dead or broken
One day, you will stand before the throne
His wind will take you, you will be blown
Away
You will have no good thing
No good words to say

The Moon Mirror

Black clouds, like drapery

Closed over the sun

At noon, sunlight, now missing

In the dark

Now just the sounds of startled birds

Fear fill those who sat in the park

The moon now appeared

Faces protruded

Next, they receded, as if excluded

There was a farce installed on humankind

The moon mirrored the earth

Seeking people would find

A mirage in a mirror of what we have here

When the unknowing learn that truth

Confusion and fear

The black drapes then parted

Those with knowledge had fun

For they knew it was coming

A revealed new sun

That was not the only sight, the next coming soon

When nighttime had fallen, we had a new moon

Signs and wonders appearing in the sky

After living so many years in a lie

The wicked ones tried to take earths control

Powerful God Almighty, again made earth whole

Love is Stronger

He could run like the wind
He wanted to be free
Women kept pursuing him
They would not let him be

He ran like a force
Today was not his day
Stronger than the wind, is love
Love always finds a way

A spark when caught by wind
Ignites into a flame
He who ran
She who sparked
In love, they are the same

Desire

Desire can play a painful game

Suppress it and it may return the same

It can overpower the thoughts in your mind

You can see everything but still feel blind

It can steal your sleep

You toss and turn

You can even feel your passion burn

Though

Desire is a gift if handled right

You can manifest your desire

Into your sight

Do not let your desire tear you apart

With prayer

God can bring the desire of your heart

Desire, desire

You can be a great teacher

I will not condemn you

Like an uptight preacher

God created you and I feel no shame

Oft times the one you desire

Desires you the same

The law of attraction makes desire grow

Do not give up on your desire

If it is from God

You will know

Your Bodyguard

Anger can be the emotion that protects you the most

It flares when you are mis-treated

It stands up when you are disrespected

It steps up to bat when you are neglected

It has a way with your emotions

When it sorts your real friends

Only in this case it is quiet

Then again it depends

Anger can make your blood boil

And boiling is purifying

It can also teach you patience

When yours, someone is trying

Anger is the emotion that can bring about love

When your forgiveness you give

Though do not use anger irrationally

Or you may cease to live

Righteous indignation is a gift to be used

It has a way of correcting

What was wrongly abused

God's Inheritance

Her heritage and its importance
Was stressed to her as a child
Though alcoholism and poor parenting
Caused that family's children to run wild
Heritage was put away
It was all but forgotten
A heritage of greater importance
She learned she was one of God's begotten
He is the greatest heritage
His inheritance has great worth
More than possessions, silver, or gold
God's own will inherit the earth
God's truly chosen, His elect
For God they will take a stance
He will give them so much more
God said, He will be their inheritance

Host with The Most

Paddy cooked the pudding hot

She put it in a shell for pie

She put it in the fridge to chill

Then piled the whipped cream high

Paddy was my kind of girl

She made few lettuce salads or rice

She cooked big meals and served desserts

All served with wine on ice

Paddy was a generous host

She fed us well; first we said grace

When God sets his table for his own

I know she will have a place

Wind of Change

In the quiet of the day
Wind starts howling, it is on its way
It has a mission to blow good in
It has a mission to blow out sin

I strain and if I listen close
I hear the words wind wants to speak
I faintly hear the forming words
The words, they come for those who seek

Change is coming with the wind
The blowing wind, a change for good
A generation is going to change
Living for God as they should
Light is overpowering the dark
The wind is blowing out a stagnant force
Retribution, stronger than the wind
As God's word rights the course

Evil's deception will be no longer
When it comes to power, God's is stronger
The blowing winds will not rescind
Till evil is gone
Blown away with God's wind

The wind, the words, the change

God's change

No more wondering why so much was strange

The wind, the wind, let it blow

God will settle the dust and we will know

Silver Stream

It is called silver stream, but the water looks gold
A silver and gold stream, with colors like stained glass
People traveled silver stream with God's invitation
To a wonderful place, where the lions eat grass

Where lions eat grass and lay down with the lambs
A place where no evil words are ever spoken
Where the glory of the Lord shines, and no one cries
A place where hearts are never broken

A banquet is prepared for those invited
Beautiful garments to be worn by all who come
A place with an atmosphere of love and joy
The invited were greeted, each one, not just some

The silver stream with stained glass and gold
God gives us His personal invitation to hold
We will travel the silver stream, till God sees our faces
With open arms He will tell us
He has saved our places

Walk Through

I walk through the frozen land
It can bring a freezing pain
Many times, I have walked through snow
Now, I walk through again

Everything in this deep snow
Nearly feels as time forgot
Though myself, I also freeze
I can forget not

It seems a blessing to feel snow's pain
At least this pain is real
Lies and deception forced on humanity
Was an invisible pain to feel

Deception's pain was felt by those
Who God gave eyes to see
Those deceived and blind to truth
Lived in ignorance, blissfully

Take A Step Back

Where did the good old days go?
Is it possible to find them again?
Somehow, they all were packed away
We have not seen them since who knows when

I remember the days, people took pride in their looks
If they were leaving the house, they dressed in care
They wore their good clothes and put on good shoes
They cleaned up and fixed their hair

Back then, people were polite and said hello
Please and thank you, where did they go?
Now if you speak, people may think you are strange
This world is getting evil, it is time for a change

If we ever find our good old days again
We need to try harder to make them stay
These bad days are becoming a living hell
I hope and pray they soon go away

Welcoming Committee

She wished she could go to the firmament
To wait for God, for whom she did live
No one knows the day or hour of his return
She hoped her impatience God would forgive
She has waited for years for his return
She loved him so much, she could barely live
She just wanted Him here for us all
Her love and a welcome, were all she could give
Our Lord deserves a welcoming committee
So, she wanted to fill that role
She hoped to be among the first to greet him
In person, not just in her soul

Treat Yourself

Your mood is off, you are feeling down

You feel you are living in crazy town

Troubles and problems are giving you a licken'

What helps you now? How about fried chicken?

Some crispy crunchy chicken fried

Mashed potatoes and gravy

Dressing on the side

Some crunchy pickles, home grown sweet corn

Some coleslaw helps when you feel forlorn

God can bless us many ways

Tasty food helps troubled days

Next time life gives you a licken'

Treat yourself to some great fried chicken

Such as These

On the road through rambling hills
Dense trees leave but a stream of sky
The trees are causing me to wonder
What is in the trees nearby

How many forests overflowing with trees?
Are waiting to be walked with feet such as these?
Where only animals have walked the ground
Grazing on foliage that does abound

Where animals graze without a scare
Unless those trees are hiding a bear
If no mountain lions are hiding in the trees
I would wander about, with feet such as these

I would walk the land, the virgin land
I would occasionally stop and raise my hand
I would wave to God, whenever I saw sky
I would tell God; here I am, I am just saying hi

I would tell God, I am enjoying your trees
Walking through with feet such as these
Looking at everything with eyes that can see
I would thank him for loving one such as me

Old Man Winter

Old man winter has come to town
It was time to let the snow come down
I am admiring the snow that fell
While others think the snow is hell
How can something so beautiful be bad?
While I feel joy, other people are mad
Old man winter's sleight of hand
Has changed the brown into white land
That is when nature takes a rest
When spring comes, all will be its best
Plants need their snow so they can sleep
I hope old man winter lets the snow fall deep
Old man winter knows how to play
When we were kids, we were out all day
We have a history, I know him well
To me he is heavenly, to others…hell

When a Strong Man Cries

It was a place a manly man did not go
He was overwhelmed to see freedom go away
He found himself in a place where strong men cried
He has never visited that place until today

He fell to his knees for the loss of freedom
Socialism happened in other countries, not here
A slippery slope to the lowest of lows
Poverty and starvation are coming with fear

Socialism was forced and it was accepted
Any rejection of it brought men to blows
That is what you can expect with Godless people
A nation's strength, stolen, while poverty grows

It was a painful process for those who knew God
They cleaved to God as their freedom died
A free country died because of the ignorant
At that time there were many strong men who cried

A war had been waged but deception ruled
Only God could help the strong ones now
Socialism had the ignorant fooled
Those who watched it happen, wondered how

Down on his knees he prayed for help

Socialism is for the most ignorant of men

Socialism is for the Godless and lazy

Socialism is evil, yes, it has always been

Later, the most ignorant of men will cry also

They will cry like babies

They will be sorry

They will cry like babies, they will cry

After the strong man cries

He will have comfort, he still has God

He will stand up and fight again

Frank and Ludmilla

It was around the year 1920
Frank asked for Ludmilla's hand
Frank and Ludmilla had to work hard
Working eighty acres of land

They started life with just a wagon
One pig, a cow, and a few small tools
A chalk rock house with just a few rooms
Back then, there were few government rules

They were not barraged with daily headaches
From a television set that brainwashed with lies
They farmed the ground and tended animals
They were not poisoned by chemtrails in skies

They did not see a world full of corrupt politicians
They did not see the evil cabal's rising power
Their food was not poisoned with chemicals
They were grateful when they could afford to buy flour

They did not see a wicked Hollywood
Full of satanic child murder and rape
They did not see the world just going to hell
Wondering if they would escape

Ludmilla grew food and worn clothes were mended
Frank planted crops and animals were tended
They dressed in their best when they went to town
They prayed and thanked God when the rain came down

Frank and Ludmilla died years ago
I am glad they are not living to see this shit show
I am waiting for God to destroy what is bad
To fill the earth with good morals...
Like my grandparents had

Silent Winter Night

A mid-December evening

The world is going to sleep

The night sky sits atop a white snow

A vision and a memory to keep

Music is softly playing

The first noel now played

I feel a lifetime of memories in this moment

As the deep snow on the ground laid

So beautiful, so beautiful

You could feel an angel's brush

Passing by to share the moment

The angel lingers, in a silent night hush

Keep Hold of My Hand

Lord, with you I will not fall
You have my heart, my soul, my hand
You are my light as I walk through darkness
My hedge of protection in a troubled land

Your shining light is erasing the night
With darkness fading, it is an easier fight
My gospel armor shines like diamonds in your light
With you holding one hand, my other has more might

Lord, I need you to keep holding my hand
I am not letting go, I am holding yours tight
You are my giant who scares the enemy
My back up if I cannot handle the fight

The Rock Tumbler

He has been kicked around like a rock
Kicked to the side or picked up and thrown
He is wearing rough edges, he is down on the ground
He had nothing to call his own

After being kicked and thrown all around
His face looked up and he looked to God
God's gentle hand had lifted him
Then God looked with a wink and a nod

God put him through His rock tumbler
To polish his rough edges and make him shine
God wanted him to know he had value
God said "you are a special rock, you are mine"

God's polish makes you feel good
He gives you more love, than anyone could
He makes you beautiful, shiny, and new
You are special to him; he is keeping you

Life Happens

Even people with tough exteriors
At times can be turned inside out
Some hardships or a tragedy
Injustices, no doubt
A person cannot live without feeling
At times, your world can be sent reeling
What was controlled and kept in place
Can put tears on the strongest face
When hurt or anger wakens a qualm
Nothing good around you can calm
It is okay to let feelings air
There will always be someone to care
We all let feelings fall outside
Feelings tough exteriors cannot hide
We put our feelings back in place
Then we soften a little, with God's grace

Remember Your Baby?

Remember the moment you held that baby
You were overwhelmed with joy
There was a pride you felt for that new life
Your new baby girl or boy

Remember your child as a toddler
Your child started hitting and sporting a bad mouth
You thought calling you names was funny
From there, it all kept going south

Remember you bought everything that child wanted
You did not want to put up with the screaming
The tantrums and attitudes and calling you names
You let your own child give you a reaming

Then your child was always rebellious
Dishing out grief to cause you pain
You could never say no to your toddler
Now your adolescent is driving you insane

You were the parent, that was your child
No discipline or rules, you let them run wild
The first time that smart mouth called you a bad name
It was your place to stop it, that brat is your blame

A generation of parents that failed
They raised their children without God
They raised self-centered spoiled rotten brats
With no guidance from God's guiding rod

A generation of self-centered young adults
With no genuine care for others
Just think of what could have been
If you were responsible fathers and mothers

The Lord is My Holiday

A holiday season is upon us once more
Now my feelings are all but gone
A sense of loyalty to the past celebrations
Yet, something inside moves on

The energy I put into previous seasons
Has changed to letting it all pass by
The affection I have cleaved to for so many years
Now just brings a sigh

There is still a feeling of nostalgia
I love the lights; I could hang them all year
The heartfelt music and songs for the season
Are pleasing to the heart and ear

I live and love the Lord so much
Seems the holidays do not compare
Though, it is the nostalgia settling in
There is still a little holiday left there

Do not Give Your Power Away

Stillness filled the air
As sullen faces ate their bread
They had nothing to live for
They lived to be fed

Then a voice spoke out
Why can't we live for more?
Opposition then spoke up
We cannot go through that door

Persistently truth spoke
We can help ourselves
We all have the power within us
We can have more on our shelves

The opposition spoke again:

We will ask the ruling class
To see what they will say
If your idea, they like not
They will give us no bread today

The truther spoke once more
Why did God go away?
We need to bring our Lord God back
We can if you believe and pray?

They wondered how they got so weak
They prayed to wait for God to speak
God said these people do not rule you
Your earnest prayers, I will see through

You see,
The government promised hope
Though you were paid in lies
Now God showed them He is their God
The weak were growing wise

Ideas grew, people grew strong
They started changing what was wrong
The ruling class could keep their bread
God is alive, He is not dead

As faith now filled the air
Happy faces, were fed God's meat
The ruling class now fed with bread
God fed them their defeat

Justice

Justice stands high on the hill
The rays of justice over the land
Beaming high up into heaven
Returning to God's hand

It returned from whence it came
It came from God and then returned
God reached out and gave it back
Because the people learned

They learned they could not rule alone
With no God, they were on their own
On their own, they failed at life
No faith in God, they lived in strife

Then people felt they had no purpose
Goodness dwindled, evil grew
They began to remember the times
When it was God who helped them through

People bowed their heads to God
They plead for mercy as they prayed
God is a forgiving God
He heard the prayers they made

Justice came with God's swift sword
His two-edged sword to cut asunder
With evil gone, no more to show
Justice rose to thunder

God is great and God is good
God's justice here on earth to dwell
The days when men thought they could rule
Made earth a living hell

God's Fire

Cinders smolder as time passes
Nothing left to keep them burning
Nothing left to stoke the fire
Nothing left for her returning
Something happened to her fire
Something no one could control
Something happened and she changed
Now her fire is in her soul
Now it burns for righteousness
No more stoking fires for men
The fire in her heart is for God
Old flames will not spark again

Snow Love

I would be standing in snow to my knees
Under billowing branches, heavily laden with snow
Where a vibration from a bird singing its song
Would persuade the branches to let their snow go
Preferably in the four or five o'clock hour
When the sky is gray with no sunset to see
That would be a memory for an evening fire
I hope someday that memory includes me
God truly blessed me to be a lover of snow
The beauty it can bring when snow falls slow
The scenes it creates under differing skies
Snow is like pure truth that makes the soul wise
The stillness snow brings when it gives the earth rest
Everything old is now beautifully dressed
Branches barren of leaves, now covered with snow
I hope I am underneath when they let their snow go

Summer Evening

It was a beautiful country day
Summer, everything green and growing
The sun was setting in the west
Only half of the sun showing

Sitting on the patio
The bugs are somewhere else tonight
I am keeping company with the Lord
With blooming flowers in sight

With cats calmly walking about
With gratitude for so much space
Thankful for the ability to work
Today, with sunshine on my face

Sunshine that seemed to be my own
It felt as if it was God's throne
Sometimes days just go your way
You cannot part with that last sun ray

It is a reward to work so hard
To work a garden and a summer yard
To sip your homemade berry wine
To spend time with the Lord, divine

Wisdom Calls

Wisdom cries out on the streets
Common sense has run away
Wisdom calls out to the fools
Though fools, they wish to stay

Wisdom says "you follied fool"
I shake my head and laugh at you
Destruction now is your reward
For the ungodly things you do

Greed and sin you wear like jewels
Proudly so, you wear your crime
Knowledge also called to you
Now you are out of time

Wisdom wearies of its calling
It called to help you find your way
If you want to stay a fool
And go to hell, you may

God's Lonely Heart Club

If you are looking for a lonely heart club

God has a lonely heart organization

He offers membership to the entire world

Every town, city, and every nation

God's mission statement is only seven words

"God will never leave or forsake you"

If you ask Him to come into your heart

You will find His mission statement is true

Jesus said he stands at the door and knocks

You can answer the door and answer his call

Now the Father, His Son, the Holy Spirit, and you

That makes four, you are not alone after all

True Friend

How quickly one can be betrayed
One little thing, there goes your friends
Now they sit in the judgement seat
That is how a friendship ends
One will judge, the rest will jury
If fortunate, one will defend
The one that does not stand and judge
That one is your friend

Shut The Door

Some doors need to be shut
Some of them should be nailed
Some should be barred or barricaded
With a concrete wall not to be failed
Hang some artwork on the wall
With a picture of a locked door
With a sign on it and the sign says
Find the missing key on the floor
No one can find the key
It is missing
That is right, the key is missing

That is what happens with false friends
They will take you to your wits ends
Your words of truth, they keep dismissing
That is why there is no key, the key is missing
They use you and snark behind your back
You can live better without their flack
Let those people go away
You will live better starting today
Sometimes doors just need to close
Who they use next, God only knows

His Son

He raised his son to be a man
From a babe, he raised him well
He raised his son to live for God
He would be there for him if he fell

He raised his son responsible
To own up to wrong things he did
He made rules to guide his son
His fatherly love he never hid

He stressed importance to work hard
No laziness, staring at screens
He raised his son to respect women
To never abuse them by any means

He taught him truth and integrity
Respect for elders, help those in need
He taught him not to be a follower
Always be willing to lead

He said, let your masculinity shine
You are a man, with that stand tall
Always keep your eyes on God
My son you will not fall

Too Many Voices

I hear the coyotes yipping
Three of them sound like twenty
Though I know they have a purpose
I think one of them is plenty
I feel the same about politicians
With their words, their meanings are many
We should only have one per state
Sometimes, I do not think we need any
It is time for a political revolution
Where the crooked learn to walk upright
Decrease politicians by ninety percent
I think we will be all right

Shade is A Shadow

Shade is a shadow

Where something has power over the sun

Where the sun cannot penetrate or overtake

And angles and trajectories

Play games for power and fun

Try to get through those branches, sun

Winter, sure, but summer, none

You can be a bully with your sunny rays

Though even the clouds can scare you, some days

You will go hide and not come out

Till the clouds change their ways

Who's Watching Who?

Outside the flowers were holding secrets

Their blooming was spectacular
Their fragrance entrancing
As I kept busy, and I was not looking
Those sneaky flowers were dancing
I said I could swear I just saw you dancing
You are all up to something; what can it be
One said we just saw your angel chasing wasps
It was your angel, and we all wanted to see

You were so busy, caring for us flowers
Your angel saw wasps, and they were mean
Your angel took charge of the situation
Your angel had to intervene
Who knew that flowers could see our angels?
They watch over us every day
How often to flowers get to see angels
Chasing wasps away

Then it was as though nothing had happened
The flowers were just flowers once more
I caught my sleeve on a thorn in the roses
My angel was not there, when my sleeve tore

Tarnish Remover

A tarnished reputation
Can be polished and once again shine
God has a special polish
The love He gives, is divine

You can look at the tarnish
You cannot see yourself showing
With some work, the tarnish dissolves
Then you look, and you will see yourself glowing

When the tarnish turns to reflection
Suddenly, your face will appear
Then God will handle you gently
He will shine you as he holds you near

Like silver, we can grow tarnished
If we do not pray, or show God we care
Though God's loving grace will shine you again
He polishes you like you are rare

The tarnish is not always our fault
External elements can grow it
You can rise above the tarnish
You can shine, God's love will show it

Checking Out Trees

A stately and handsome pine
Pleasing to walk by
Though admire this one from afar
Or get poked in the eye

Those well-formed hawthorn trees
Pleasing to behold
Yet, keep your distance, do not reach out
You may find thorns to hold

A beautiful weeping willow tree
What a vision to be found
Though when it is time to change the season
There is a real mess on the ground

A purple leaved white birch tree
A lovely vision to see as I strolled
An attractive shape, white papery bark
Many birds, its branches will hold

Some people are like trees
Nice to look at, nice qualities
Though there is more than meets the eye
You can stop or just walk by

My favorite tree, the tree of life
This rare tree, there is only one
This tree gives eternal life
This tree, He is God's son

Soldier for The Lord

He sat upright in his rocker
The rocker moved, just tiny rocks
He looks somber, mostly staring
He is focused on the ticking clocks

Not the clocks that hang or chime
He minds the clocks inside his head
He needs more time to right the wrongs
Time's running out, it is time for bed

He has some projects he is working on
He wants to fix our world's affairs
He wants to help fix a crooked system
It is a mess and then he swears

He is a soldier for the Lord
While he rocks, he prays and plans
He tells God, this is not His mess
It was not your fault Lord, it was man's

Halo of Feathers

She wore a halo of feathers
She would wear her halo till she gets her crown
Her halo had feathers from birds she loved
With a little bit of ribbon and a little soft bird down

A beautiful feather, for accepting Christ as her Lord
A few more feathers for all she had achieved
A few special feathers for prayers that were answered
A few were God's blessings, because she believed

It was a halo only her and God could see
She lived for God and always tried her best
When she receives her heavenly crown
She will put her earthly halo to rest

God's Cheerleaders

Lord, when you are ready to start judging our enemies
If you want any cheerleaders, to cheer you on
I will be in the crowd with your loving admirers
We will be with you, till our enemies are gone

Give me an H and an E and an L and L
These guys raped kids, Lord, send them to hell

Here is a good one Lord,
They worshiped Satan, that is not a joke
Make Satan worshipers go up in smoke

Lord, how about…
Make the flames go higher and higher
Let evil doers burn in the lake of fire

Lord I am just saying I am here for you
With so much evil, you have a lot to do

Far be it from me to step on toes
Or where not wanted, insert my nose
The least we can do is shout some cheers
As you throw the wicked out by their rears

Chocolate Secret

I will marry a chocolatier
I will ask him to bring samples home
I will love him very much
I know for sure, I will never roam
I love chocolate, dark or milk
Covering nuts or smooth as silk
In bars or drops or in a box
Even candy covered chocolate rocks
I will marry a chocolatier if I can
I will always love my chocolate
(Oops), correction, my man

Windy Visit

She enjoyed banter with the wind
They found each other both amused
She said "thanks for blowing some people away
It is better to be alone than used"

The wind enjoyed the banter as well
"It is my pleasure to blow them off
I am glad you do not beg for relationships
With selfish people who mock and scoff
You found a friend with me, I am strong
We blow off people who do not belong
We let them close and give them a chance
But find they were not worth our glance
It is a troubled world
That is why I blow
To cut things loose that need to go
And we blow them off
We blow them away
People we do not need
Or wish to stay"

The wind said "step outside
If you want to talk
I will not blow hard
I will just visit as you walk"

Happy in The Now Space

The past is gone, the future unknown

Today is the day that we can own

Every minute that you live

Think of ways that you can give

You can be happy all day long

If something happens that is wrong

Do not give in and wear a frown

Do not be depressed and do not feel down

Never start a day with a chip on your shoulder

That chip could turn into a boulder

Just let things go, and let them be

Forgive all grievances, set them free

Just live happy everyday

Living happy In the now space

That is God's way

I Know This Tree

God is like a tree with falling leaves
His words are piling on the ground
He sheds them to help others see
The ones who come around
People who search, they are few
Though often comes a passerby
His beautiful words continue to fall
So beautiful, when piled high
A rare soul searches for the truthful word
This soul finds God's words piled like leaves
Gathering them forever more
With truth and God, that soul now cleaves

Get The Rake

The tree glowed with orange leaves
I stood in awe at the righteous tones
This tree stood a king amongst trees
With the sun slipping as dusk hears man's groans
Put the machinery away, dear
It is cold out here without my long sleeves
Take a good look at that tree dear
Soon, you will be raking those leaves

Larry and Rose

They called her symphony Rose
She hit the low notes when she spoke of her woes
She hit the high notes whenever she froze
Orchestra Larry wants to marry her, she knows

People called him orchestra Larry
He wrote love notes for his beloved Rose to carry
He wrote her love songs, asking her to marry
Larry did not want Rose to tarry

Larry and Rose were instruments of love
When Larry held her hand, she wore a lace glove
His latest composition gave her that shove
She accepted, and God blessed them with music from above

In time, their duo became a quartet
She bought a canary, he got a dog for a pet
He helped compose her; no more would she fret
They made great music together, babies? Not yet

Counting Fake Feathers

Fixing a stolen election

It was like butchering chickens

With a plastic picnic knife

Some states used a toothpick

To butcher the chickens

Do not forget, they did it blindfolded

Painful for the chickens

People grew weary of the prolonged process

It should have been swift and merciful

Use a sharp axe dammit

Clenched teeth and a grimace

Painful for good people to endure

Prolonging the result

The states had a lot of chicken feathers to count

They were not all chicken feathers

Lots of fake feathers

The people behind this

Should be tarred and feathered

Stay Busy Not Lazy

She sat alone with her thoughts
They kept her busy as well
Idle hands are the devil's workshop
She did not want them reaching for hell
The more you do, the more God gives
She stays busy because He lives
She lets her hands work to the Lord
Someday she will reap her reward
Some people may fear judgement day
Though God's judgement is not one way
You get what you have coming to you
If you love God, you receive rewards
If you do not, you are through

Accept The Invitation

The tables were set for God's invited
A beautiful wedding party, prepared by the Lord
Though everyone had received invitations
Many looked, and the invitations, ignored

The Lord said go and search the streets
Bring all without an upturned nose
His servants found the poor and downtrodden
The unloved and lonely and such as those

The table of the Lord is great
The grateful people were seated and ate
Those who snubbed God endured a fate
They did not want God yet, they wanted to wait

The humble and the lesser came
They were grateful God had called their name
God's invitation was not a game
Though newly called, God loved them the same

With arms wide open, God accepted them all
Those who wanted Him and heard his call
God's chosen walked to the banquet hall
Those who refused God were now blocked by a wall

Look Beyond Seeing

To look beyond what man can see
Unknown to man, but sight for the soul
It is God's wisdom I am searching for
To know all things of God, my goal

Wherever I look, I see God's ways
Towering trees or water that falls
Stones too heavy for man to lift
Timely steady rain that falls

The snow that falls and lays to shine
With moonlight catching glitter frozen
Someone such as myself, Lord
To feel unworthy and find myself chosen

To see the sky, turn so many colors
Mountain ranges that sit atop land
Waters so beautiful in tropical colors
Those colors bordered by warm white sand

I have nothing to compare to your ways
Our Father in heaven, you created it all
I just have my love, my prayers and praise
They have been yours since I first heard you call

Clarence

Put the bottle down, Clarence
Your kids are wearing ragged clothes
Your wife is lonely raising those kids
She is getting mental, and it shows

Find another pastime, Clarence
Upkeep on your house or cleaning your yard
You could spend time with your family
For a grown man, these should not be hard

You have a terrible pastime, Clarence
You should just go home after work
Your wife's mental health is slipping away
Only, where there is a new woman, you lurk

What are you telling the priest, Clarence?
You go to confession and think all is well
After confession, you go to the bar for communion
While your family just goes to hell

Full Moon

If it feels like one of those days
It is all nettles, brambles, and thorns
Weeds, cockleburs, and every red light
Smiles have been hijacked by scorns
The full moon wreaks havoc with the lunatics
You feel you are in an episode of the twilight zone
Put on a slight smile and do not look around
The loonies will leave you alone

Going Downhill

It was a poverty of spirit
A country growing poor of God
An abundance of secular living prevailed
A war on God and God's word assailed
Killing babies by abortion was hailed
As a society goes to hell

There was a draught of faith
Many had no faith in God
They fought Him and pushed Him far away
They hoped no one talked about "God" today
They raised their children Godless, and Godless were they
As a country slid into gender hell

To hell they will go if they do not turn around
To hell they will go, lest they answer the door
Jesus is still knocking
The clock is tick-tocking
Now Jesus tires of knocking his knuckles on your door

Stop killing those babies and calling it health
Start worshipping God and stop worshipping wealth
Get off your drugs and get your gender straight
Hell is waiting with a wide-open gate

Satan already has a hold of your hand
With an evil grip you can barely stand
He is not pulling you in for a party
There are no parties in hell and what is more

Jesus stands at your door, and He is knocking
He loves you and soon there will be no more tick tocking
It is time to get up and answer the door
Do not go to hell... answer the door

Two is Company

If false friends are better than no friends
I would prefer to be alone
I will just walk the narrow path
With the only real friend I have known

The path I once thought was lonely
Is the path I now walk everyday
Traveling with you Lord, by my side
I will stay on your path all the way

Two is company, three is a crowd
Though, there is always room for a new friend
I will keep a little room between me and you Lord
In case you find someone to send

Horse Smiles

Well, you like the fellow fine
He is a decent guy, well-meaning but wrong
You do not agree with him, though you are still polite
Today, you just want to get along

Just throw your head back
Show a toothy grin
Do not tell him what you are thinking
Today, keep that within

Today you can take his words in stride
You can just ignore his style
Afterall, he is only a man
Even a horse can smile

Changing Instruments

He played the piano and she cried
It was as if he knew what she was feeling inside
Those were the chords that her heart could not find
She wanted the piano man
She left her country music husband behind

The next one played the electric guitar
He got the closest to her soul by far
When he played, her eyes closed, and she bowed her head
Her piano husband's eyes bulged
When the divorce papers were read

Next, she left him and his electric guitar
Chuck, the drummer in the band, was the coolest so far
But all he did was smoke pot and play his drums, what a bummer
She was weary from that life
She divorced her drummer

Well, she has left her fourth husband now
She has had four husbands, she wondered why and how
She went to a lounge and when she got inside
Number two was there; he played the piano and she cried

This time, he did not want her by his side
He did not even want to take her for a ride
He said, "hell no" and he pushed her aside
She got what she deserved, and she cried

Pebbles to Mountains

Mountains standing strong
Pebbles have power too
A pebble can stop a moving force
If it gets in your shoe

With the greatest faith
Mountains can be moved
Just as a pebble stops a force
The latter, easier proved

God said faith can move mountains
I say common sense ends pain
I will stop and dump this pebble out
Then work on the mountain again

Feeding The Soul

God's word is like an overflowing field
Bursting with food, so that many can eat
To feed their hearts, souls, and minds
They all start with milk and then move on to wheat

As they feed and grow in God's word
God offers more, they move on to meat
God sets a table with everything good
He always invites you to take a seat

God's word is ever growing
What God offers will feed every need
Whether it is milk, wheat, or meat
You will find it, in His words you read

Water Trees

Real trees were looking at water trees
Asking, what beautiful trees are these?
Those are us, growing near the mirrored lake
How beautiful we are, for heaven's sake

The trees were whistling in the strong breeze
How can these whistles come from us trees?
It is nature's music, from branches and wind
The trees whistled a silly tune, and I grinned

There is something mysterious, the trees by the lake
The real trees cast a vision for the water to take
The real trees can keep secrets or whistle in the breeze
The water trees are magic, they disappear as they please

Clouds of Birds

Dear Lord, please bring clouds of birds
Guide them to my trees to stay
Cardinals, orioles, chickadees
Finches that do not go away

Bring meadowlarks, and more blue jays
Bring sparrows, robins, and juncos too
Woodpeckers, doves, and little wrens
Hummingbirds, a hundred will do

Also, Lord, bring butterflies
Every color and every size
Bring enough to fill my skies
When it is dark, send fireflies

One thing more I ask of you
Let the birds just eat birdseed
I do not want the birds to catch
Or eat my butterflies for feed

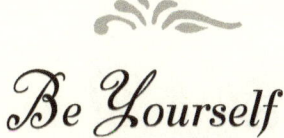

Be Yourself

He was like an ocean liner on a river
Everything he did, was in a big way
He tried to make a way where others could not
He lived bigger than life, some would say

Occasionally, even big ships will find
They need smaller boats to give them a hand
The little guy will pull him back into the water
When he gets stuck or hits some dry land

Ocean liners, belong on the ocean
Traveling waters where they belong
Occasionally, you will see a tugboat working
Helping the ocean liner, who was in the wrong

The Slow Down Gift

People scurry
Like pigeons walking fast
Hurry! Hurry!
Heads bopping to and fro
They had to hurry to get things done
Fast, they had to go

They had to hurry to this place
They had to hurry to the next
They want to hurry
Fast! Fast! Fast!
Hurried, they were vexed

When they were home
They could not rest
They had no peace
North, south, east, west
They did not know
Christ was their King
They ran fast to everything

One thing all these did not know

If they found Christ

Their fast would slow

God would show them how to go

His love would help their fast to slow

God would help them slow their stride

They would feel peace

With Christ inside

Gentle Love

The wind displayed its gentle side
It found hearing ears to confide
It blessed them with a gentle breeze
To put their hearts and minds at ease
For even though it could blow strong
They knew to God they did belong
God's great love will reassure
It tells things to hearts that are pure
To those who love me, blessings flow
They follow you where you will go
Their hearts will wear my words inside
Like priceless jewels, they will not hide
Words from God, the wind will give
To those who love God, they will live

Stir The Flame

He was salty

She was sweet

He wore boots

She liked bare feet

He liked country

She liked rock

She liked his truck

But liked to walk

Now love will spark

Sparks can cause flames

If handled right

The fire tames

Fed with fuel

That keeps it burning

They found love

Open to learning

Differences, akin to spice

Kept the fire

Burning nice

She loved him

He loved her

Now and then

You need to stir

The fire

Oh-No

The gentle breeze had turned to wind

The wind then full of blowing dirt

The dirt was lies to blind the eyes

It is dishing out more hurt

Oh-No!

So much dirt gets in your eyes

You rub them to remove the lies

You find the media's lies are not true

Now truth is finally coming through

Oh-No! Oh-No!

You have become wise

Your eyes have opened to the lies

Put on your shades, to see what is true

No longer will the blowing lies hurt you

Grab The Tailwind

Now the wind said "grab my tail"

I will pull you up above the lies

I will take you to a truthful place

You will have new ears, you will have new eyes

Ignore the politicians' words

Good-bye athletes and Hollywood

I will show you a life far better

Those you idolize are not good

The wind says you are better than these

Rise above and you will be free

That is what tailwinds are for

They will pull you up so you can see

Politicians' words are dung

Celebrities have no control

Mainstream media is gushing with lies

Ignore them all, and mind your soul

Grab the tailwinds my dears

Hold on tight and you will find

The wind is God's, and it brings truth

You can leave the lies behind

It is Good to Be Home

It was time to get out and about

The journey was to some local stores

A discovery was made, there was nothing to miss

Home came the bags and next lock the doors

It is crazy out there

Really crazy out there

People wearing masks

They are under control

They do not fight

They just give up their rights

First their rights

Next their soul

It was great to be back home

It was wonderful to be home

Celebrate Honesty

I can feel my spirit soaring

When I see justice being served

When you can see the bad guys getting

Exactly what they deserved

In a world full of corrupt lawyers and judges

We can still find honest men

Though they are rare and harder to find

I would say one in ten

When you find that one beacon

A man to keep the law upright

You can praise God and celebrate

For these days, that is a rare sight

Really Real

Flat earth with ice around its diameter
With a firmament dome to protect the earth
I do not have trouble seeing it
I am a flat earther, for what it is worth

I know there are continents hidden away
A mystery hidden and not yet known
Is that where the so-called aliens live?
Is there life, like our own?

I wonder if they have it all together?
Where they live in peace, with Christ as their King
Hopefully, they do not have politicians
No politicians would be a wonderful thing

Could those unknown continents hold the garden of Eden?
God closed it and hid it many years ago
Hopefully soon, flat earth truth will come out
We will all be astonished when we know

God said eyes have not seen, nor ears heard
Nor have entered the heart of man
The things that God has prepared for those who love Him
Can I imagine a flat earth? Yes, I can

The Greatest Shelter

Living for God
Is like living in a safe shelter
When rain falls cold
When skies are dark
When thunder speaks
After lightning strikes
When winds blow hard
When hail falls
When you are pounded in like spikes
When blizzards come
When snow falls deep
His love protects and is yours to keep
God is protection from the storms
His love is like a fire that warms
He is our fortress, safe and sound
He gave us Jesus Christ now crowned
Lord of lords and King of kings
Protecting you, from all life brings

Mourning Coffee

She was pouring the mourning coffee

After his death, the people came

She was more a solitary person

She did not feel the same

She only wanted to be alone

Visitors did not understand

She had to smile and serve refreshments

While no one gave a hand

Strangers came and filled her house

To mourn and visit and take her time

It was an awkward time for her

Again, she heard a chime

Oh, yet another guest

Some poor soul she barely knew

They sat and drank their mourning coffee

While she wanted a brew

She did her duty, she let them in

To reminisce and mourn and grieve

She finally had her own house back

Relieved they all did leave

Now cold beers were calling her

She will mourn in her own way

The chapter of this book is now closed

Tomorrow is another day

The Cardinal's Song

I wake to hear the Cardinal's song

He had a song to share

I turned from my side to my back

To listen and to stare

His song though sweet, it had a sadness

He is calling for a mate

Nature now is prompting him

There is no more time to wait

I have seen her here. She hears him call

When it is time to nest

She stays put, but for a season

Then leaves to take a rest

The Cardinal's song, natures design

To call to find bird love

I also wait for the call

When the Cardinals, I think of

End The Movie

Even the wind grew tired of the show

At the drive-in theater, it began to blow

The movie, never ending

The popcorn gone

The people were weary

They wanted to move on

End the shit show once and for all

Put the truth out

I heard the curtain call

The ruling class kept the truth hidden

The actual truth had become forbidden

The guardians of the truth now

Had been directing a show

It was painful, long, and slow

Here comes the wind, it is time to blow

Time for every lie to go

Speak up, yell down, scream in or out

Speak the truth or let it shout

No more lies

Now end the show

It is time to let the people know

Just put the truth out

Let it be

It is late now set the people free

The wind was disgusted and blew down the screen

To me, that was the greatest scene

Respect for The Elderly

The windbreak stood like an old folks gathering

Crooked trees, broken, some had bare tops

It looked like it was a leaving this earth party

Respectfully, still the wind stops

So many battles, the wind, and the trees

The wind now stops before the stand

For even while the old trees are dying

Their roots still hold the land

Soon, there will be new little soldiers

More trees to grow to fight the wind

For now, the wind with utmost reverence

For the old trees, will rescind

No Rain

Draught can cause a heart to grieve
The rain has stopped, why did it leave?
The death of rain, it will not fall
The rain refuses to hear earth call

The ground calls out with clouds of dust
In pain it cracks, rain is a must
You pray and grieve and even lust
For rain to fall, you have even cussed

No rain, no showers, just dry pain
You long to feel it fall again
Empty winds just bring disdain
Draught causes some to go insane

It is a travesty, to be so dry
Inside, I try to reason why
My heart and soul forecast a cry
Though tears will not fall
They are standing by

Praying Late

I am taking the night watch tonight

Sleep is elusive when prayers need praying
Who can sleep, while devils need slaying?
Sweet dreams are calling, but they will have to wait
I have so many prayers, I will be up late

The early birds can have their worms
I am choking the devil, and he really squirms
I am praying to God for evil's demise
It depends how late I am up when I will rise

Lord, the devil is getting thrashed
By praying your words, he is getting smashed
I am putting a prayer whipping on his game
Lord, give the devil a heaping of shame

Not too many people are up late with God
I have His attention till I start to nod
I am on the night watch with prayers to pray
Hopefully tomorrow is a better day

Be Well Rooted

I came upon a fallen tree
It once stood to touch the sky
Now it rests atop the earth
No more will it stand high

There are people like the trees
The heights they reached as fortunes grew
Though some had reached too high too fast
Like trees, they can fall too

It is best to start by growing roots
Roots that grow deep to then spread wide
Then you can grow to touch the sky
And take life's storms in stride

The Wings I Loved

Sadness looked upon the wings
The soul of a feathered love, now gone
A beloved companion has passed away
The beautiful wings, now tears fall on
Chitters and chatters and even some screams
Have flown into memories, and later, my dreams
With a hope that one day in the promised land
Those beautiful wings will fly back to my hand

Beautiful Wine

She was staring at her wine

God's words had warned her not to stare

Do not marvel at the color

Or drink so much you glare

Sip a little for your health

Do not indulge in ample measure

You may fall into temptation or

You may find illicit pleasure

She would heed the words of God

She, His faithful, did obey

To honor Jesus who made miracle wine

When she sips her wine, she will pray

Gust

I was taking a stroll and joking with the wind
The wind asked "do you know my little brother Gust?
Gust does not have the stamina I have
But he can perform when he feels he must
He is somewhat of a showoff
He enjoys causing shock and awe
He incorporates some Coriales force
Along with Newton's law"
I said "I know some people who can act that way
They force their effect on you
Then they blow away
Sometimes they damage you
If you are strong, you still stand
And you laugh and flip them off
With the middle finger on your hand
I have my own force
Who protects me from this kind
But thank you wind for your company
And leaving your brother Gust behind"

Walk Slow

Walking on a faded road

It has been abandoned for a while

Time and chance have brought me back

What comes to mind? A smile

I left this road not to return

Now love has sparked, I will let It burn

A little fire, is now a flame

I remember the rules of this game

I have love to stoke the fire

To fuel the flame to burning higher

I enjoy the feelings now awake

And

I will give him my love and his I will take

No Thank You

Another serving of disappointment
Heavily scooped to fill my plate
No thank you, I will pass for now
I will close my eyes and wait
I have been stuffed full of disappointment
Anymore and I will burst
I hoped and prayed for something better
Time and chance gave me the worst
The only bright side I can see
Is God is watching over me
I can handle what comes my way
Though today is not good, please stay away

Slippery Slope

Sometimes, you find a slippery slope

Your feet may slip, you reach for hope

One-foot slides, while one stays firm

You slip and slide over a worm

Worms are troubles that appear

You wonder how your foot got here

Sliding, you ask God for strength

To make steps of a goodly length

God will take those troubling worms

Those slippery things that cause the squirms

He will send them back where they belong

God corrects steps that were wrong

Then strong you will climb and strong you will stand

Do not take the slide, just take God's hand

Snow Geese

Ribbons of snow geese descend from the sky
Swirling to land on a field nearby
Caught up in a process of nature's design
White with black wing tips, the sight is divine
How many miles have these travelers flown?
Tame they would be if they were my own
I would walk through the masses, admiring them all
I would look in their eyes, they would come when I call
I would reach out my hands when their beaks reach to me
I would touch them and bless them, that is how it would be
Amid the thousands of traveling birds
I would look at them smiling, reciting God's words
Even though they try to repeat what I say
They just keep honking and that is okay
They are just geese, and they honk, and they fly
When God calls "Come now birds," I will wave them good-bye
Just another wonder of God's own design
For a moment in time Lord, I felt as though they were mine

The Gift of Love

His arms were strong, embracing her

He kissed her and she felt a blur

Her knees were weak, but he was strong

He kissed her hard, he kissed her long

No hurry now to end the kiss

Love waited many years for this

Love had to wait to be God's way

He chose them for this love today

Dear Lord, he is strong inside and out

He was her other half, no doubt

She was trembling, he was strong

Their love never would be wrong

Answered prayers, God heard them pray

True love will always find a way

Ascending

She climbed a stairway in her mind
Ascending to new heights to find
God is luring her so high
His invitation drew her nigh
She found His goodness, peace, and love
Good things she finds from God above
I am closer Lord; I hear you speak
I am stronger now, no longer weak
The light that shines with love, I find
It soothes the heart, the soul and mind
I will not be taking those stairs down
As I ascend to see Christ's crown
Your justice Lord, shines on my face
The steps I climb, each a new place
I am finding treasures on my way
Even more so when I pray

Oldie but Goodie

He was in his winter years

A snowy top, too old for fears

He has seen it all

He has done it too

His days are dwindling

To a few

A year, a month, a week, a day

Only God knows that today

Snowy top, he is not dead yet

Telling stories, you cannot forget

His stories keep your eyes and ears

A couple times, they came with tears

You shake your head and say "oh my"

To see the twinkle in his eye

The laugh that comes with what was said

Sometimes you laugh till you are red

The love you feel is on his face

His hands then fold, now touched with grace

You return home and silently pray

Dear Lord, do not take him, let him stay

Compassionate Wind

A different wind came with compassion

For the lonely hearts, the ones that ache

It slows and touches those souls gently

Subduing as if there was a windbreak

The gentle touch that travels through

Is God's own spirit, it is for you

Embrace the breeze and if you can

Hear the words God gave to man

He can bring love to the lonely

To some, He is their one and only

Praying on your feet or on your knees

For those, God has a special breeze

It brings love to those who stay

It blows the loneliness away

Blackbird Leaves

Blackbird leaves on bare spring trees

Blackbird parties on the ground

Robins return by the hundreds

Gleaning what can be found

Now the finches come to feed

They disappeared from here last fall

Spring has sprung with feathered hope

They heard the return call

Happily, they sing to spring

To wake the dormant trees and earth

With joy they wake the sleeping season

It is Spring, time for new birth

The Show

The wind blew in, the veil lifted
A show was playing for the gifted
We all laughed and ate popped corn
To see a new age being born
We saw the end of child rape
Abusers punished, no escape
Politicians lost their standing
Accountability, folks were demanding
Roles changed for celebrities
No more would athletes take their knees
No more did people want these roles
Their lives were changed
They now had souls
Truth prevailed in every scene
The wind? It was not always mean
It made us laugh; it made us pray
Grateful, it blew evil away
Alas, the ending blew us away too
The end was the beginning for me and you
New worlds opened for us to see
We were in awe; how could this be
God is great, he is true, and good
We loved His show, we knew we would
Now it was us who took the stage
As we now lived in a new world age

Truth Seeker

She found herself in that place again
How she got there was hers to know
That internal voice was calling her
Again, she had to go
This time it was for clarification
For things she knew but could not prove
Mountains could not stop her now
She would make them move
No, it was not a deep dark place
She stood in the brightest light
Answers could be found by seekers
She prayed for what was right
She sought the one who paid the ransom
Through Him all blessings would flow
Be still, and know that I Am, He said
She was patient and wanted to know
This time the words were not for sharing
They were hers to keep and hold
Words from God all to herself
More valuable than gold

Invisible Wind

There is a wind you cannot feel
Delivering words that come from God
I stand receptive to the hearing
I stand like a lightning rod
God is searching for receptors
His eyes are fixed on those who hear
Though unworthy I find myself
He calls me worthy and keeps me near
God's words come in a timely manner
They soothe my soul and keep me calm
They give me strength; they give me love
God's forgiveness, a healing balm

ℋold 𝒴our 𝒱ision

I held a vision and destiny responded
I overcame tests and challenges
With God's grace

When my resolve was tested
I focused on my vision
In God's divine timing
He let love find its place

When the darkest moments
Cannot become any darker
Your innermost faith will shine your way
I held my vision of receiving true love
Now my vision is here to stay
My vision manifested and God brought me true love
He lights my darkness and makes me whole
Never give up when you have a vision
Especially when you feel it deep in your soul

Killing Flowers

I slowly watched my flowers die
The wind blew hot, the wind speeds high
Poor flowers never had a chance
To show their beauty or breezily dance
Though I watered them so well
The wind wreaked havoc, even hell
What a disappointing thing
No joy, would this year's flowers bring
So much hard work and planning here
God said "you know how I feel, dear"
"My people, who I called and chose
Did not produce a single rose
The elements of life and sin
Saw to it I cannot let them in
When things in this world got too hot
They turned from me and called me not"
I hear you God, but they had souls
My flowers only had my goals
Though Lord, I sure know how you feel
We hurt from loss, that hurt is real
The wind brought great loss to my plans
Your loss Lord, was not yours, but mans

Be Strong

Afterall, the wind was right

It was God who spoke the light

It was God's power that caused the blowing

A special wind that brings the knowing

All those with hearing ears took heed

God speaks to them when there is a need

All those who had eyes to see

Saw the same things God showed me

The wind had power to change the ways

Of those who lived ungodly days

Though the wind was strong

God's patience long

He used His force to change what was wrong

Take heed when God's wind you hear speak

It is meant to make you strong

Not weak

The End

Oh gee, the wind is still blowing...

Though I feel a shift...

Love is coming....

This love is glowing

www.ingramcontent.com/pod-product-compliance
Lightning Source LLC
Chambersburg PA
CBHW030304130626
46549CB00002B/688